The Art of Making Paper Flowers

By

Robert and Jane Morris

The Art of Making Paper Flowers
©2008 Robert Morris and Jane Morris
All rights reserved.

PREFACE

Years ago, I learned to make paper flowers from my mother. Crepe paper flowers were fun to make, and made a cheerful addition to our home. The flowers were inexpensive and the materials were readily available.

Nowadays people seek crafts they can enjoy without a huge investment. You may want projects you can do with your children. You may want to decorate for a party, or for each new season, without spending an arm and a leg.

Whatever your level of artistic ability and crafting skill, you can enjoy making these flowers. Making crepe paper flowers is a terrific family activity. In fact, groups of all kinds can enjoy this craft. You could entertain senior citizens at an activity center or a rest home; they are sure to remember this craft from their younger days. But young people, such as Scout groups, will also enjoy it.

In this book, I have updated all the instructions to take you step-by-step through process of making each flower. You can start with easy projects, such as the Marigold or the Bunch of Violets, and work your way up to more difficult projects, such as the Large Rose. Or, you can dive right in, because my instructions make every step clear.

Please read Chapter 1, which explains the materials you will need and teaches you techniques you will use over and over again. Chapter 2 gives you many suggestions for using crepe paper flowers.

The remaining chapters are instructions for making 15 flowers. I have alphabetized them according to the name of the flower, so that you will find instructions for large, medium and small roses following one another.

You may copy the patterns and instructions for your personal use or for a group activity. All other uses are protected by copyright.

I hope you have the same joy and satisfaction as you create your flowers as I have in helping bring back this craft of yesteryear.

Robert Morris
Jane Morris

TABLE OF CONTENTS

Chapter 1 – Materials and Techniques . . . . Page 3

Chapter 2 – Using Paper Flowers . . . . Page 15

Chapter 3 – Apple Blossom Spray . . . . Page 19

Chapter 4 – Aster . . . . Page 25

Chapter 5 – Calla Lily . . . . Page 30

Chapter 6 – Leaf Spray . . . . Page 36

Chapter 7 – Marigold . . . . Page 39

Chapter 8 – Poinsettia . . . . Page 41

Chapter 9 – Memorial Day Poppy . . . . Page 47

Chapter 10 – Oriental Poppy . . . . Page 51

Chapter 11– Crushed Rose . . . . Page 57

Chapter 12– Large Rose . . . . Page 59

Chapter 13– Rose . . . . Page 66

Chapter 14 – Shell Flower . . . . Page 73

Chapter 15 – Tulips . . . . Page 76

Chapter 16– Bunch of Violets . . . . Page 81

Chapter 17– Water Lily . . . . Page 84

Materials and Techniques

Many readers will want to skip this chapter and dive right in. But, please, do read through it. You don't want to be in the middle of a project and discover you don't have everything you need to finish it. Especially if you're working with children!

Of course, you don't have to memorize the chapter. It's going to be here whenever you need to refer to it.

You may have many of the materials you need already. If not, you can find them at your local craft store, on the Internet, or even (for some items) at a "dollar store." Don't be afraid to try different tools to achieve the effect you want. Just don't get the paper wet unless you have tested it to be sure it doesn't run!

The techniques you will read about in this chapter are used over and over again in making paper flowers. Simply refer to them, as you need to, according to the instructions for each flower.

Materials

Making paper flowers requires a few materials and tools. We have listed first everything you will need for all the crepe paper projects, then everything you will need for the tissue paper projects. Then, the tools and materials that are required for some, but not all, the projects are listed, along with items that are optional.

Caution:

Remember that the coloring of crepe paper and tissue paper sometimes runs. Test a small piece by dipping a corner in water. If it does run, be sure your hands and work surface and tools are completely dry before you begin. Keep your paper flowers away from water. The color in the paper will run onto anything it touches if it gets wet.

To make the crepe paper flowers in this book, you will need:

- Crepe paper in the colors you select for the flowers. The instructions for each flower will specify whether you need duplex paper, which has doubled sheets, or plain (simplex) crepe paper.

    It is available in craft stores in packets of large folded sheets. In preparing this book, we found only plain (simplex) crepe paper in a limited range of colors. You may have a little difficulty finding crepe paper.

    However, you can find crepe paper streamers in many places and in a wide variety of colors. You can use the streamers with any pattern that will fit as long as you pay attention to the grain lines. You can always use streamers to wrap stems. Crepe paper streamers are usually about 2" wide.

- Floral tape for stems. You can use crepe paper, but floral tape is neater. Use green floral tape to wrap flower stems and brown floral tape (if you can find it) for wrapping branches.

- 20-gauge wire for stems. Thick florist's wire will work well.

- 28-gauge wire for wiring leaves and petals that need a little extra "body." Thin florist's wire works well.

- Craft glue or white glue. The glue must dry clear.

- Brush for applying glue. If you apply glue straight from the container, you may apply too much. If you use your finger, you may tear the crepe paper, which becomes more fragile when it is wet.

- Small sharp scissors. Scissors work best. Using punches or craft knives may stretch the crepe paper.

- Wire cutter for stems. Don't use the scissors you use to cut paper because the wire will dull them or even make small notches in the blade.

- Quilter's plastic to make templates. You can use any relatively heavy clear plastic that you can cut with scissors. You can also copy the pattern, cut out the copy, and trace it onto cardboard. The cardboard should be about as heavy as an empty cereal box, so you can get a nice, clean edge.

> ***Note: You can use tissue paper to make some of the flowers in this book. Read the directions. If you do not need to stretch petals or stretch leaves, then you can use tissue paper. If the petals must be bent, then wire two layers of tissue paper following the directions for Tulip leaves.***
>
> ***Be sure to test tissue paper by dipping a small piece into water to determine whether or not it runs.***
>
> ***You should be able to use a punch with tissue paper, since stretching is not an issue.***
>
> ***Paper with a single color makes more realistic flowers, but do not be afraid of darker colors. Since the flowers are not always realistic, experiment with tissue paper that has a small pattern.***
>
> ***Don't be afraid to combine papers, using crepe paper for the petals, for example, and tissue paper for the leaves.***

Some projects may require:

- Knitting needle, skewer, chopstick or other thin rod to roll the edges of flowers.

- Ball over which to shape petals, such as a Styrofoam ball or other ball to fit the petals.

- Stapler.

- Hairspray. Test it on a small piece of crepe paper to be sure the color does not run.

- Wax. Paraffin works best, but you can also use scrap candles if they are pale in color. For some flowers, you might want to experiment with tinted wax.

- Scented oils to suit the flower you are making, or a "mixed bouquet" type of scented oil. For short-term scent, you can try perfume, but test the perfume on a scrap of paper to be sure it does not run.

- Pinking shears or other decorative scissors.

- Artificial stamens. You can often make the stamens with paper, but the pre-made ones do look nicer.

- Micro beads and double-sided tape.

- Coloring and decorating materials as described below.

Techniques

In this section, you'll learn some techniques that you can use over and over again. You can refer to these instructions whenever you need to in your adventures with paper flowers.

> ### *Caution*
>
> ***These techniques use sharp scissors or wire. Be sure your children know how to use them safely, and supervise them while they use these techniques. Otherwise, steps that require scissors or wire should be done by adults.***

Making and Using Templates from Patterns

If you are making just one flower, you can copy the pattern in this book on a copier or with tracing paper, cut out the copy and use that as a template.

If you are making more flowers, you will probably want a more "heavy duty" template.

The Art of Making Paper Flowers

You can make a good template using the plastic that quilters use for appliqué. It is clear, so you can trace the pattern through it. It is easy to cut cleanly.

And, it is heavy-duty so it will last for many, many flowers. Just follow the instructions and remember not to get your paper wet (use a pencil).

The plastic used to make your own stencils will also work well.

You can substitute any plastic that you can see through and cut cleanly with either your scissors or a craft knife. Just trace the pattern in the book onto the plastic. Remember to draw on your template the parallel lines in the center of the original pattern. Cut out the template and you're ready to go.

You can also use cardboard templates. They cost nothing, and last long enough for most projects. (And it's easy enough to make another one.) You can use any thin cardboard—from a cereal box or other food box, for example.

1. Cut a good-sized piece from your box.
2. Copy the pattern from this book on a copier or with tracing paper and pencil.
3. Cut out the copy.
4. Use a pencil to trace around it onto your cardboard.
5. Cut out the template from the cardboard.
6. Add the lines as they are shown on the original pattern.

Please remember that the patterns in this book are protected by copyright. You have permission to copy them only for your own use.

Changing the Size of Patterns

Do not limit yourself to the pattern sizes given in this book. You can make smaller flowers, perhaps to use in a doll house, or as part of a corsage. And, you can make bigger flowers to make a big statement in your décor.

If you are using both leaves and flowers, remember to re-size the patterns for the leaves, too.

The easiest way to change the size of patterns is to use a copier. Just use the enlargement setting on the copying machine. If you visit a copy shop, the attendant can show you how, but it is really simple.

- If you want to make a bigger pattern, use a bigger number on the enlargement setting. For instance, if you set the enlargement to 200%, you will get a pattern that is twice as large as your original.

- If you want to make a smaller pattern, use a smaller number on the enlargement setting. If you want a pattern that is half the size of the original, for instance, set the enlargement to 50%.

If you have a computer and scanner, you can also scan the pattern and use any graphics program to change its size.

Many of the patterns in this book are simple enough that you can get a satisfactory change in size by tracing or copying them, and then drawing freehand either inside or outside the lines to make a smaller or larger pattern.

Remember to add the grain lines in the middle of the pattern.

Cutting Your Pieces

Crepe paper has what seamstresses call "bias." It stretches more easily in one direction or the other. If you look at a piece of crepe paper, you will see a "grain" like the grain in wood. Try to stretch the paper in the direction of the grain. Not much give, is there? Now try stretching it across the grain. It is that stretch that lets you make realistic paper flowers.

The pattern pieces in this book all have 3 solid lines in the middle of the piece. When you lay the pattern pieces on the crepe paper, be sure the lines are on the grain (parallel to the wrinkles).

If your crepe paper came folded in a packet, take care so that you do not cut pieces that will have a fold in them. You cannot remove the fold marks and they will ruin your flower. Some instructions ask you to place the pattern on a fold line; in that case, follow the instructions because the fold marks will not matter.

To cut pieces one at a time:

1. If your template does not have the grain lines, add them now.

2. Lay the template on the paper with the lines on the grain and trace around it.

3. Cut out the petal or leaf.

To cut many pieces at once:

1. Without fully unwrapping your crepe paper, slide enough crepe paper out of the sleeve so you can lay the template on it and have an inch or so on top and bottom.

2. Put the template on the paper with the lines on the grain. Draw a rough square about an inch out from the template on all sides.

3. Staple along the square so all the thicknesses are held together.

4. Put the template down again and draw around it with a pencil.

5. Cut out the shape.

6. This may seem wasteful of paper, but it saves a lot of time. If you can fit two templates onto the same section of paper, do them both at the same time.

Using Florist Tape or Crepe Paper to Make Stems

You can buy florist tape in green, brown or white. Select the color that best suits your project.

The Art of Making Paper Flowers

If you are using crepe paper, you must cut strips against the grain of the paper so it will stretch. The simplest way to do this is: keep the paper in its sleeve and slide the whole roll of paper so that a half-inch or so of the paper peeks out, and then cut your strip.

You can also use a crepe paper streamer. With the streamer still in a roll, just unroll a bit and cut it right up the middle with your scissors. Cut a yard or

more at a time; you will need about that much to wrap a stem. You will have two strips, each about 1" wide.

1. Use wire cutters to cut the 20-gauge wire to the length you need according to the directions.

2. Using the whole roll of florist tape or the whole strip of crepe paper, hold the end of the paper or tape and the wire between the thumb and forefinger of your left hand.

3. If you are using florist tape, unwind about ten inches of tape and give it a tug. Stretching the tape activates the adhesive that is built into it.

4. Twist the wire and tape or crepe paper with your left hand while pulling gently with your right hand so the wrapping spirals neatly down the wire.

5. Stop to add leaves, by holding the base of the leaf onto the wire in your left hand. Continue to spiral the wrapping over the leaf base. A dab of glue will help secure the leaf.

6. At the end of the wire, tear off the tape or paper and roll the end between your thumb and forefinger to "smoosh" the cut end into the stem. (You may need to glue the end of the crepe paper.)

This technique takes a little practice, but soon you will be spiraling down the wire in just a few seconds. Honest!

Adding More Color to Paper Flowers

Crepe paper comes only in solid colors, but natural flowers often have several shades and hues on petals and leaves. If you like, you can use various media to color your creations and give them a more natural look.

It is much easier to add color to the various parts of a flower before it is assembled, when you can work with flat pieces of crepe paper. You can always make a sample to see where you want the color to be.

If you use crepe paper whose color runs:

One easy way to add color variation to your flowers is with water. Put a little water on a brush or on your fingertips and sprinkle on some scrap crepe paper. If you like the effect, use it on your flowers.

If you dip one end of a petal in water, and then put it between sheets of blotting paper, you get a shaded effect.

These coloring materials work with any crepe paper:

Artist's pastels work well to apply shading and color variation to paper flowers. You will want to seal them with the spray that is made for that purpose. You can buy both the pastels and the sealant at large craft stores or at artist's supply stores.

If you have watercolor paint, use your finger or a brush to remove color from the dry paint and apply it to the crepe paper.

Try using powdered rouge or eye shadow. Test it on a scrap first. Use your finger or a brush to apply. Be sure the make-up won't run in water (some brands may run).

If you are sure your crepe paper is waterproof:

Use magic markers to color the crepe paper.

You can also use watercolors as you normally would (with water and a brush.) You can use water-based ink, too.

Be careful with any paint or ink that contains alcohol. Test it on a scrap, because "waterproof" does not mean "alcohol-proof."

Waxing Flowers

Waxed paper flowers were very popular in Victorian times. You may like this special finish, especially on flowers that have thick leaves, such as lilies (including water lilies and calla lilies).

You can use Duplex crepe paper, though the colors will be somewhat muted. Simplex crepe paper works better, and is more readily available. Start with

large flowers without a lot of detail. If you like the effect, you can experiment on other flowers.

You can use flowers that have been tinted with artist's pastels. If you want to wax flowers that have been tinted with another medium, test first.

Because you are going to dip the whole flower into the wax, you need a finished flower. You also need enough wax so that you can dip it without wrinkling it.

For the wax, you can use white or pastel candle stubs, or just buy a few candles at the "dollar store." White, green or blue shades work best for leaves and stems. Other shades "muddy" the green color. Break up your stubs and candles and take out the wicks. If you are using stubs, avoid getting the burnt bits of wick into your wax.

Caution

- ***Be sure the container for your melted wax is dry. Water in wax causes splatters that can burn you or cause a fire.***

- ***Always use a double boiler for melting wax. Otherwise you may have a serious fire.***

- ***If your wax begins to smoke, remove it from stove right away. It is about to burst into flame.***

- ***Only adults should work with hot wax.***

Now you are safe to begin:

1. Check that you have plenty of water in the bottom of your double boiler.

2. Put smallish chunks of wax into the top of the double boiler and let the boiling water below melt the wax.

3. Use a candy thermometer to measure the wax temperature. You want your melted wax to be 130 degrees Fahrenheit. If you don't have a thermometer, take a piece of crepe paper and dip the bottom into the wax. If the paper shrivels, the wax is too hot. You want a fine coating of wax on the paper.

4. When the wax is the correct temperature, turn off the heat.

5. Hold your finished flower by the stem and quickly dip it in and out of the wax. Take care not to burn your fingers.

6. Carefully shake the flower over the wax bath to get rid of excess wax. Use a toothpick to remove any globs of wax that stick to the center of the flower. Don't worry about small areas that are not covered, or are too thick. You are going to dip again.

7. Separate any petals that have stuck together, and remold any petals that have lost their shape.

8. Let the flower cool for ten minutes or so. Stand the flower upright so the waxed petals do not deform under pressure.

9. Repeat the dipping and cooling process until you have a finish you like. As you continue dipping, the wax will cool. If it drops below 120 degrees Fahrenheit, you must heat it a little. Your last dip should be at 120 degrees Fahrenheit or a little warmer.

You can also apply wax with a brush (a basting brush works). You can spoon wax over the flower, leaves and stems in thin coats. Spooning or brushing works well for waxing stems and leaves.

Other Finishes on Flowers

Spraying several light coats of hairspray on your finished flowers gives them an almost porcelain appearance. BUT, you must read the ingredients on the hairspray can. If your hairspray contains water, don't use it with crepe paper whose color runs. Cheap hairspray from the "dollar store" usually works better than more expensive sprays. Always test a piece of crepe paper first, and remember to test each color of crepe paper you have used in your flower. Hairspray will not make your flowers waterproof.

At your craft store, you will find a product designed to give a porcelain look to paper. You may want to experiment with this finish.

If you have a favorite sealant used to cover chalk or for clay and paper clay, try it on a test scrap of crepe paper.

"Mixed Media" and Paper Flowers

You may find that floral tape works better than green crepe paper for wrapping stems. In the same way, if you have some sprigs of silk greenery, you can add them to your crepe-paper-flower bouquet. Feel free to use artificial leaves—but do be sure they are the right size for your flower.

Micro-beads are very tiny, hole-less, glass beads sold in craft stores. You can use them to enhance your flowers wherever the flower will bear their weight—usually in the center of the flower. They are applied using double-sided tape. Glue will not hold them very well, but if they are not going to be held very much you might try experimenting with different glues that dry clear.

You can also "dust" your crepe paper flowers with fine glitter or with metallic or colored powders. You may need a very, very fine layer of glue to hold these substances in place.

USING PAPER FLOWERS

> ***CAUTION:** Wherever you use your beautiful paper flowers, remember that they are not always waterproof and may bleed their color onto anything they touch if they get wet! Always test your paper, and only use waterproof paper if it may get wet.*

Paper flowers are an inexpensive way to highlight colors in your decorating color scheme. You can make arrangements to suit the season or the occasion without spending an arm and a leg.

Paper flowers add an authentic note to Victorian décor. Victorian ladies would have made large bouquets that featured many different flowers. They collected exotic flowers with a passion, and they enjoyed handcrafts of all kinds. Their bouquets were a riot of color and texture, each unique and reflecting the personality of its creator.

If you love things retro, then paper flowers are for you! In the 1930's, 40's and 50's, homemakers brought some cheer into their homes with crepe paper flowers. Times were hard, and crepe paper was inexpensive. They found many inventive ways to use the flowers they made. Nowadays quilt shops carry fabric that mimics the colors and patterns of those bygone days. You could visit a quilt shop to see what colors and combinations were used.

Crepe paper flowers do not need to look "natural" to be beautiful. You can make a flower whose shape you love in any color that suits you. You can use different shades of the same color for leaves or for petals. You can apply color and shading in a variety of ways, as described in Chapter 2.

No matter what style of home décor you prefer, crepe paper flowers set your imagination free. You can put them into a variety of containers. You can use them in places that real flowers would never fit. And, you can use them on a variety of occasions. Here are some ideas to get you started:

Containers

Arrange roses in a teapot. You needn't throw away a cracked teapot, or one without a lid. Use it for a centerpiece even if you don't serve crumpets!

If your favorite vase has cracked, you can still use it for paper flowers.

It's very hard to make an arrangement with live flowers in a shallow bowl. You can do it with paper flowers.

1. Decide how high you want the arrangement to be.
2. Gather the flowers you want to use into a bunch. You may want to include some artificial or crepe paper greenery, especially at the outside of the bunch.
3. Fasten the bunch with wire or a rubber band just below the height you want the arrangement to be. Fasten the bunch so it is loose enough to allow the stems to slide a little; then you can vary the height of the flowers in the arrangement later.
4. Bend the stems out in all directions at right angles (close is good enough) just below the fastening. This will make a secure base for your arrangement.
5. Put the bunch into the shallow bowl; cut off any stems that are too long or twist the stem until it fits into the bowl.
6. If you want a permanent arrangement, hot glue the stems to the bottom of the bowl. If you want to re-use the bowl, use a washable glue.
7. Now bend and slide the flowers and stems until the arrangement pleases you.
8. Tuck florist's moss into the bowl to hide any visible stems.

Make a "woodsy" arrangement by hot-gluing flowers to a branch. A flower-decked branch set on a mirror makes a lovely centerpiece.

Places

Put flowery garlands above doorways and windows, or to highlight special pictures. Use the wire stems or hot glue to fasten crepe paper flowers onto swags. You can use twigs or branches, raffia, ribbon, fabric or artificial greenery to make the swags.

The Art of Making Paper Flowers

Keep a bouquet in the guest bathroom. You can use a drop of essential oil to scent the bouquet.

Use crepe paper flowers as drapery tie-backs. Just wrap the stem around the drape to hold the drapery in place.

Glue a magnet to the back of a flower to hold notes on your refrigerator.

Adorn picture frames by gluing on appropriately sized crepe paper flowers.

Decorate your Christmas tree with crepe paper flowers. They can burn, so keep them away from lights.

Glue crepe paper flowers to gift wrap, or on a gift bag. Dress up a gift of wine with a flower. Just wrap the wire stem around the neck of the bottle. (Add another piece of wire to hold the flower's head up, if need be.)

Use hot glue or wire to add crepe paper flowers to any wreath base: straw, wire, grapevine or artificial greenery.

Use short-stemmed flowers for corsages and boutonnieres. (You can make flowers smaller by reducing the pattern on your computer or on a photo-copier.)

Glue tiny flowers to a plastic headband for a child.

Glue crepe paper flowers to a straw hat to wear on sunny days.

Occasions

Put a crepe paper rose in a bud vase when you serve Mom breakfast in bed for her birthday.

Serve a birthday tea for little girls and their dollies. Use crepe paper flowers for the centerpiece, for place cards and for garlands for each celebrant's hair. (To make a hair garland, just use the stems to weave flowers into a circle, being very careful to curl any poky wire end into loops so they cannot hurt anyone.)

The Art of Making Paper Flowers

Make white, red or pink poinsettias for wreaths and garlands at Christmas time. Sprinkle them with glitter for extra pizzazz.

For a bridal shower, make some of the flowers the bride has chosen for the ceremony. Or, make any flowers you like from white crepe paper.

- Use the flowers as centerpieces and for place cards.
- Strew crepe paper flowers on the gift table, using washable fabric glue if you must keep them in place on the cloth.
- Let the bride sit under a canopy decorated with crepe paper flowers.
- If the guests don't know each other, make corsages for each, gluing crepe paper flowers to a small card so their name peeks out at top or bottom.
- Place bouquets where guests leave their coats and in the guest bathroom.

Crepe paper flowers are perfect for a baby shower. If you know whether the baby will be a boy or a girl, you can make all types of flowers either blue or pink. Make a centerpiece by gluing toy blocks into a pleasing shape and then wiring on or gluing on paper flowers. Or make a small bouquet for a teddy bear to hold!

Using silver or white crepe paper and lots of glitter, decorate with crepe paper poinsettias for New Year's.

Make green roses or poppies for St. Patrick's Day fun!

Every month has a birthstone. Use the color of the gem when you make crepe paper flowers for centerpieces, place cards and gift wrap. Be sure to use real icing for flowers on the cake!

Whether you've invited a crowd for a major milestone, or have dinner for two, you can make crepe paper flowers for your anniversary party. Use some of the flowers you used on your wedding day to bring back memories. You might make a simple corsage and boutonniere, or a simple centerpiece. If you've rented a hall for a large party, crepe paper flowers let you put a bouquet on every table. Decorate an arch under which the happy couple can repeat their vows.

These suggestions should spark your own creativity. Remember to send your ideas for the newsletter.

APPLE BLOSSOM SPRAY

These directions make a 24" spray of apple blossoms. You might decorate window valences with them, or hang them over doorways. Put several sprays in a tall vase to welcome spring. You can make shorter sprays, or fasten the blossom clusters to a headband for a little girl.

You will need:

Brown crepe paper for stems (or brown floral tape)
Green crepe paper for leaves
Yellow crepe paper for stamens
White or pink crepe paper for the flowers
Scissors
Wire cutter
Ruler
White glue or craft glue

Brush for applying glue
Florist's wire, 20 gauge for stems, 28 gauge to wire flower together
Floral tape, brown (optional)

Real twigs 4" or 5" long (optional)
Real branch or brown wrapped wire from craft store
Cut out pattern pieces or templates

> **Note: Because you need so many flowers and leaves to make a spray of apple blossoms, this is a good time to use the technique for cutting out several pieces described in Chapter 1. Remember to cut a calyx for each flower and each bud.**

> **Note: Skip this section if you are using artificial stamens.**

Make the Center of the Flower

1. From the yellow crepe paper cut a strip 3/4" wide (with the grain). You will need about 1" for each flower you plan to make, so if you want 30 flowers, cut the strip 30" long (against the grain).
2. Stretch the strip fully, holding on 3/4" edge in each hand and pulling gently until the crepe paper has no more "give."
3. Fold the paper to a manageable size and cut very narrow fringes, about 1/2" deep.
4. Cut off a 1" piece of fringe.
5. Apply a bead of glue along the uncut edge of the strip.
6. Gather the fringe along the bottom edge so you have a tight bunch.
7. Pinch the bottom (glued) edge together tightly and twist it to secure the flower center.
8. Repeat steps 4 through 7 for each flower center. You will need one center for each flower, 30 for the whole spray.

Make the Flower Components

1. From the white or pink crepe paper, cut the strip of petals, paying attention to the grain lines. For the whole spray, cut 30 strips.
2. Cup each petal on the strip by holding the petal between your thumb and forefinger at the widest point and pulling gently to make the petal "balloon" slightly.
3. From the green crepe paper, cut one calyx for each flower from the smaller calyx pattern (No. 1); you need 30 for the whole spray.
4. From the green crepe paper, cut one calyx for each bud from the larger calyx pattern (No. 2); you need 20 for the whole spray.

Make the Buds

1. Cut two 6" pieces of thin (28-gauge) wire. Make tiny loops at each end for safety and straighten the wires.
2. Cut a strip of brown crepe paper 1/2" wide (with the grain) across the whole packet of crepe paper to use for wrapping stems.
3. From the white or pink crepe paper, cut a strip 1-1/2" wide (with the grain) and 4 long (against the grain).
4. Cut a square piece, 1-1/2" by 1-1/2," from the white or pink strip.
5. Wad the rest of the strip into a ball about 3/8" across.

   - Roll and squeeze the strip into a ball. Roll it between the palms of your hands, as you would cookie dough.
   - Glue the loop on one piece of wire.
   - Gently open the ball slightly and insert the glued loop. This wire will be the stem of the bud.
   - Hold the ball with the wire tightly for a few seconds to allow the glue to set.
   - Glue any outer edges of the ball that do not lay flat.

6. Wrap the ball with the square of pink or white paper:

   - Lay the square flat on your work surface and put the ball in the center of the square.
   - Cover the ball lightly with glue.

- Hold the ball in place (use the wire) and bring one corner of the square up and across to the center of the ball.
- Continue to hold the ball and bring the opposite corner up and across to the center of the ball.
- Bring the remaining two corners up and across, one at a time.
- Wrap the second wire around the bottom of the covered ball and down the stem to fasten.

7. Wrap the calyx around the base of the ball so the points go on top of the pink bud and fasten it with glue.
8. Using the brown crepe paper or floral tape, wrap the stem as described in Chapter 1.

Make about 20 buds for the whole spray.

Assemble Each Flower

1. Cut a 6" piece of fine (28-gauge) wire.
2. Apply a bead of glue along the uncut edge of one petal strip.
3. Gather the petal strip loosely around each yellow flower center, with the round petals about 1/2" above the fringed stamens.
4. Apply a bead of glue to the base of one of the smaller calyxes.
5. Wrap the calyx around the base of the flower.
6. Arrange the petals to look like an apple blossom.
7. Fasten the petals and calyx by wrapping the 6" piece of fine wire around the base of the flower. Begin wrapping near the middle of the wire. The extra wire will form the stem.
8. Using brown crepe paper or floral tape, wrap the stem as described in Chapter 1.

Make 30 flowers for the whole spray

Assemble Flower Clusters

1. Cut 1 or 2 leaves for each cluster. If you make 3 clusters, you will need about 6 leaves.
2. Make a bunch of 2 to 5 flowers and 3 or 4 buds, with the tops all even. Vary the number of flowers and buds in each bunch.
3. Beginning about 2" below the base of the flowers, wrap all the stems with brown crepe paper or floral tape adding 1 or 2 leaves about 1/2" after you begin wrapping. Pinch a pleat into the leaf base and wrap it around the stem; then wrap over the pleat.

Assemble the Spray

If you have a real branch, simply fasten the clusters at intervals along the branch in a realistic way. Spread flowers and buds within the clusters in a natural way. Otherwise:

1. Cut lengths of fine (28-gauge) wire 8", 10", and 18" long.
2. Cut a length of heavy (20-gauge) wire 24" long or use brown wrapped wire.
3. If you have real twigs, attach each one to fine wire (28-gauge) by wrapping with brown crepe paper or brown floral tape.
4. Wrap each twig a second time, adding blossom clusters 3-4" apart.
5. If you have brown wrapped wire, bend it into natural curves. Affix the blossom clusters, one at the end and then a few inches apart, by wrapping with brown crepe paper or brown floral tape.
6. Otherwise:

   - Wrap the heavy wire with brown crepe paper until it is nearly as thick as a pencil.
   - Use brown floral tape, if you have it, for the last layer of wrapping.
   - As you add the last layer, add the blossom clusters, one at the end, and then a few inches apart down the stem.

7. Bend the twigs and the flowers and buds within the sprays into natural positions.

Petals:

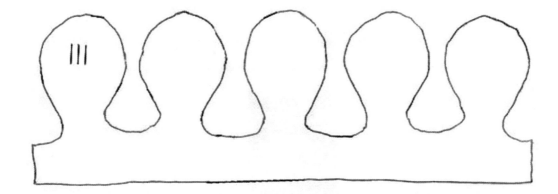

Calyx:

Leaf:

The Art of Making Paper Flowers

ASTERS

In nature, asters come in a variety of colors, especially blues and pinks. But feel free to create your crepe paper asters in any color you like. They look great in a bouquet. They also make a wonderful boutonniere. If you make a boutonniere, omit the leaves and make the stem about 3" long.

You will need:

Green crepe paper for leaves and stem
Colored or white crepe paper for the asters
Scissors
Wire cutter
Ruler
Craft glue or white glue
Brush for applying glue
Floral wire, 20 gauge for stems, 28 gauge to wire flower together
Floral tape (optional)
Cut out pattern pieces or templates

Make the Center of the Flower

1. From the flower-colored crepe paper, cut a strip 2" wide (measure with the grain) and 5" long (measure across the grain).
2. Cut a 14" length of 20-gauge wire for the stem. Use your fingers to make tiny loops at each end for safety. Straighten the wire.
3. Gently stretch the paper, holding one 2" end in each hand, until it looses all its "give."
4. You will make a fine fringe 5" long. Cut straight lines 3/8" deep and as close together as you can to make the fringe.
5. Apply glue to the top 1" of the 14" length of heavy wire.
6. Add a bead of glue to the straight (bottom) edge of the frings
7. Roll the strip of fringe into a tight bunch around the glued wire.
8. Secure the bunch with a dab of glue. If necessary, trim the top of the fringe so it is even.

Make the Leaves and Calyx:

1. Cut a 10" piece of 28-gauge wire, straighten it to remove the "bumps," and use your fingers to make a tiny loop at each end to prevent poking yourself.
2. From the green crepe paper, cut a strip 1/2" wide (with the grain) and at least 2' long to wrap the leaf stems.
3. From the green crepe paper, cut 6 or 8 leaf shapes to make 3 or 4 leaves. Pay attention to the grain lines. You will put 2 leaf shapes together to make each leaf.
4. Make a leaf by sandwiching wire between 2 leaf shapes. Repeat these steps for each leaf:
   - Make a thin line of glue down the middle of one leaf shape from the top of the shape to the bottom.
   - Lay the wire on the glue, with the extra wire sticking out of the flat bottom of the leaf shape.
   - Lay the second leaf shape top of the first one, carefully matching the sides.
   - Weight the leaf-wire-leaf "sandwich" with a heavy book and let the glue dry for a few minutes.
   - Little by little, lift the sides of the top leaf shape and apply a line of glue to the outer edge of the bottom leaf shape.

The Art of Making Paper Flowers

- Carefully press the top leaf shape to the bottom one, making sure the edges match. If the edges do not match, trim with your scissors.
- Weight the leaf-wire-leaf "sandwich" again and let it dry.
- Wrap the stem with green floral tape or with a 1" wide strip of green crepe paper as described in Chapter 1.

5. For the calyx, cut a piece of green crepe paper 1" wide (with the grain) and 2" long.
6. Cut to make a strip of fringe 2" long with each cut 1/2" deep and 1/4" apart.
7. Snip each piece of the fringe so that it is pointed at the top.

Make the Petals

> ***Note: Your flower will look more natural if you do not trace the patterns, but cut petals freehand in the approximate size and shape shown in the patterns.***

1. From the flower-colored crepe paper, cut 2 strips, each 2-1/4" wide (measure with the grain) and 5" long (measure across the grain).
2. Fold one strip of paper in half, to make a piece 2-1/2" long and 2-1/4" wide.
3. Lay the pattern for the large petals on the fold so one side edge of the pattern is on the fold.
4. Trace the pattern and cut or cut freehand. Now you have a 5" strip of petals.
5. Gently curl the petals over the blade of a scissors, just as you would curl ribbon. Aster petals arch out and down from the flower center.
6. Using the pattern for the smaller petals, and the second strip of crepe paper, cut and curl the strip of smaller petals.

Assemble the Flower

1. Cut a 1" strip of green crepe paper, using the whole package as described in Chapter 1.
2. Cut a 6" length of 28-gauge (fine) wire. Make a tiny loop at each end of the wire for safety and straighten the wire.
3. Gather the strip of smaller petals around the flower center. Be sure the petals do not hide one another. If you must, cut the

strip and start wrapping it again in another spot. Be careful not to twist petals from a previous row.
4. Do the same thing with the strip of larger petals, gluing as you go.

Note: You might find it easiest to wrap the petals if you hold the center by the stem wire with the center hanging down.

5. Starting on the outside, bend the petals so they curl down and away from the center. The petals should be shortest close to the center and get larger with each row out from the center.
6. Using the 10" length of 28-gauge (fine) wire, tightly wrap the bottom inch or so of the flower and continue wrapping down the stem.
7. Attach the green calyx, wrapping it around the base around the base of the flower,
8. Using the 1" strip of green crepe paper, wrap it around the 20-gauge wire to form the stem as described in Chapter 1.
9. Wrap again, using floral tape if you have it, or more 1" wide green crepe paper, adding the leaves 2 at a time on opposite sides of the stem, with the first pair 2" down from the flower and the second pair 2" down from that. To add a leaf, pinch the base of the leaf into a pleat and wrap that around the stem, then wrap.

Note: If you will use the flower flat, cut the stem to about 3."

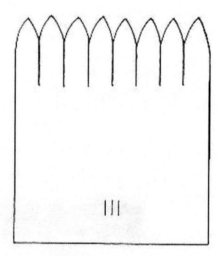 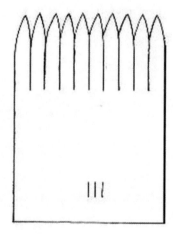

Small Petals

The Art of Making Paper Flowers

Leaf

CALLA LILY

The calla lily is simple and elegant. It can be used alone, or as part of a bouquet. In nature, callas are white or subtly colored in purple or rose shades. You can try making the calla larger, for a more emphatic decorating statement.

You will need:

Green crepe paper for leaves and stem
Yellow crepe paper for stamens
White crepe paper for flowers
Scissors
Wire cutter
Ruler
Pencil
Craft glue or white glue
Brush for applying glue
Florist's wire, 20 gauge for stems, 28 gauge to wire flower together
Floral tape (optional)
Microbeads, yellow (optional)
Double-sided tape (optional)
Cut out pattern pieces or templates

Note: The calla leaves and petals are large. Be sure you do not have a fold in the crepe paper when you cut them. You will never be able to get rid of the fold.

Make the Leaves:

1. Cut a 14" piece of 20-gauge wire, straighten it to remove the "bumps," and use your fingers to make a tiny loop at each end to prevent poking yourself.
2. From the green crepe paper, cut a strip 1/2" wide (with the grain) and at least 2' long to wrap the leaf stems.
3. You will glue together 2 leaf shapes to make each leaf, so you need 2 or 4 leaves for each flower you plan to make. Cut at least 2 at a time, so the pairs of leaf shapes match when you glue them together.
4. Make a leaf by sandwiching wire between 2 leaf shapes. Repeat these steps for each leaf:
   - Make a thin line of glue down the middle of one leaf shape from the top of the shape to the bottom.
   - Lay the wire on the glue, with the extra wire sticking out of the flat bottom of the leaf shape.
   - Lay the second leaf shape top of the first one, carefully matching the sides.
   - Weight the leaf-wire-leaf "sandwich" with a heavy book and let the glue dry for a few minutes.
   - Little by little, lift the sides of the top leaf shape and apply a line of glue to the outer edge of the bottom leaf shape.
   - Carefully press the top leaf shape to the bottom one, making sure the edges match. If the edges do not match, trim with your scissors.
   - Weight the leaf-wire-leaf "sandwich" again and let it dry.
   - Wrap the stem with green floral tape or with a 1" wide strip of green crepe paper as described in Chapter 1.

Make the Center of the Flower

> ***Note: If you are making more than one flower at a time, make all the stamens at once. Otherwise, you will have extra "confetti," which will make a mess of your workspace.***

1. Cut a 1/2" strip of yellow crepe paper the across the width of the whole packet as described in Chapter 1.
2. Cut a 15" long piece of 20-gauge (heavy) wire. Straighten the wire and use your fingers to make tiny loops at each end for safety.

3. Apply glue to one 1/2" end of the yellow paper. Apply it to the top 1/2" end of the wire and continue to wrap the yellow crepe paper around the top 3-1/2 inches of the wire until the wrapped piece is 1/4" in diameter to make a stamen. Use dabs of glue to secure the crepe paper as you wrap. Be sure the loop is covered.

> **Note: You are about to make confetti, which will be glued to the stamen to look like pollen. The smaller the pieces of confetti you make, the better the pollen will look. You can affix Microbeads to the stamen with double-sided tape and skip the next steps.**

4. Cut a 3" strip of yellow crepe paper through the whole thickness of the packet as described in chapter 1.
5. Keeping the crepe paper in its original layers, cut slits in the crepe paper very, very close together and about 1/2" deep.
6. Cut across the slits to make tiny pieces of confetti.
7. Cover the yellow stamen with white glue. A brush will help you apply the glue smoothly and not too thickly.
8. Roll and press the stamen into the confetti. Use your fingers to add more confetti until the stamen is thickly covered.
9. Set the stamen aside to dry.

Make the Petal

1. Cut out the single petal. If you want to color it, now is the time to do so.
2. Apply glue from the base to about 3" up from the bottom along one slanted side of the petal.
3. Keep the glued surface up. Carefully, and without creasing, bend the glued side toward the center of the petal. Hold it there while you fold the unglued side of the petal on top of the glued side, overlapping about 1/4" at the bottom, and tapering the overlap to nothing to make a petal that looks like a calla bloom. You can use the closed blade of your scissors as a backing when you press the two sides together.

> **Note: Calla flowers and leaves are good candidates for waxing, as described in Chapter 1. Dip the leaves as described, but after the first dip or two, use a brush to coat the flower, to avoid too much wax on the stamen.**

Assemble the Flower

1. Cut a 5" piece of 28-gauge wire, straighten it, and use your fingers to make tiny loops at each end.
2. Drop the stamen, wire-end first, down the center of the flower and hold it so that the top of the stamen is 1/2" above the spot where the two sides of the petal are first glued together (the "V" shape in the front of the flower).
3. Wrap the 5" piece of 28-gauge wire tightly around the base of the flower to secure it.
4. Using floral tape or green crepe paper, wrap the stem until it is at least 1/4" in diameter. Wrap in the leaves with the last layer of wrapping so the top of the leaf is about 1/2" lower than the base of the flower.
5. Find the pointed tip opposite the lowest part of the flower. Roll the tip into a vertical point by holding the crepe paper between your moistened thumb and forefinger and gently rolling the tip.
6. Always stretching against the grain of the crepe paper, gently stretch the top edge of the flower, and down the sides to the beginning of the "V" shape.
7. Curl the stretched part of the flower over a pencil and roll them back into the shape shown in the photograph.
8. Curl the lower edges of the leaves over a pencil and then bend the leaf stems slightly away from the flower as shown in the photograph.

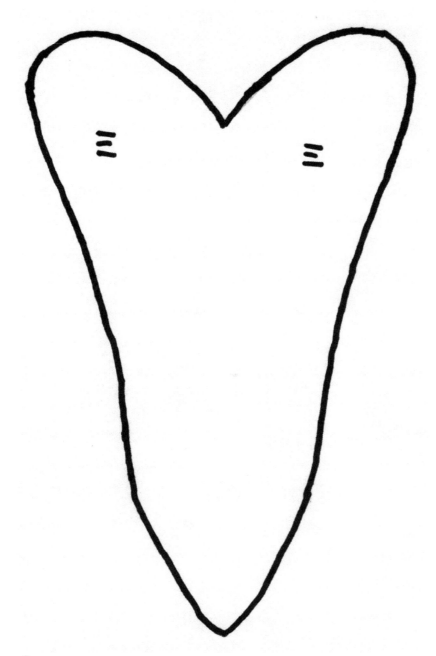

Leaf

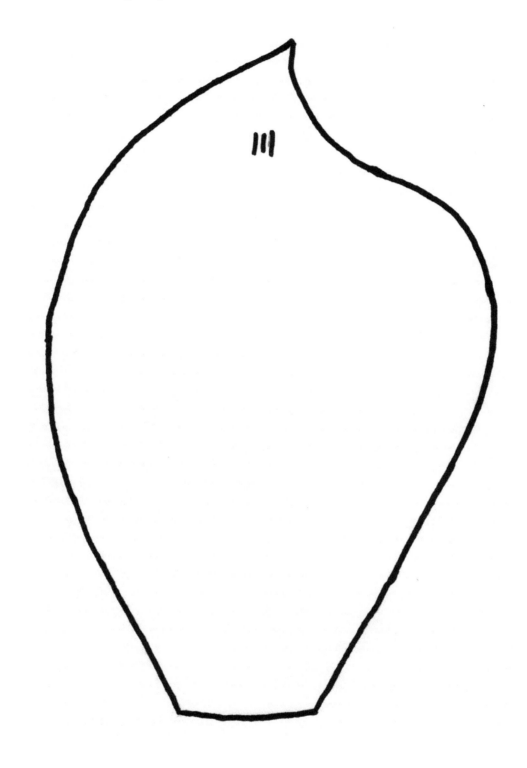

Petal

LEAF SPRAY

Most bouquets look more beautiful with extra greenery. You can make single sprays, or wrap several small sprays into a larger "branch." You can also reduce or enlarge the pattern to make leaves of any size you like. You can use two shades of green, putting one shade on the top of the leaf, the other on the bottom. Experiment by making sprays using leaf patterns from various flowers in this book.

You will need:

Green crepe paper for leaves and stem
Scissors
Wire Cutter
Ruler
Craft glue or white glue
Brush for applying glue
Floral wire, 20 gauge for stems, 28 gauge for leaves.
Floral tape (optional)
Cut out pattern pieces or templates

Make the Leaf Sprays:

Note: This is a good time to use the technique for cutting multiple pieces described in Chapter 1.

1. Cut 5 10" pieces of 28-gauge wire, straighten them to remove the "bumps," and use your fingers to make a tiny loop at each end to prevent poking yourself.
2. Cut a piece of 20-gauge wire 18" long, straighten it and add loops at each end.

3. From the green crepe paper, cut a strip 1/2" wide (with the grain) and at least 2' long to wrap the leaf stems.
4. From the green crepe paper, cut 12 leaf shapes for each spray, paying attention to the grain marks. You will put 2 of them together to make each leaf.
5. Make a leaf by sandwiching wire between 2 leaf shapes. Repeat these steps for 5 leaves:

    - Make a thin line of glue down the middle of one leaf shape from the top of the shape to the bottom.
    - Lay the wire on the glue, with the extra wire sticking out of the flat bottom of the leaf shape.
    - Lay the second leaf shape top of the first one, carefully matching the sides.
    - Weight the leaf-wire-leaf "sandwich" with a heavy book and let the glue dry for a few minutes.
    - Little by little, lift the sides of the top leaf shape and apply a line of glue to the outer edge of the bottom leaf shape.
    - Carefully press the top leaf shape to the bottom one, making sure the edges match. If the edges do not match, trim with your scissors.
    - Weight the leaf-wire-leaf "sandwich" again and let it dry.
    - Wrap the stem with green floral tape or with a 1" wide strip of green crepe paper as described in Chapter 1.

6. The sixth leaf will be at the top of the spray. Make it the same way as the others, but use the heavy 20-gauge wire.

7. As you wrap the stem of this last (top) leaf, add the first leaf about 4" down from the top one, and add a leaf every four inches below that. The leaves should be opposite one another. To add another spray, add the new spray instead of the last leaf.

The Art of Making Paper Flowers

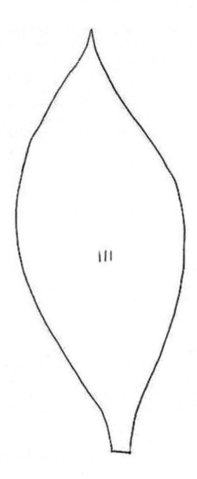

MARIGOLD

The marigold is one of the easiest flowers to make from crepe paper. You can use it in bouquets for a bright touch of color. And crepe paper marigolds have an advantage over real ones – they don't smell!

You will need:

Green crepe paper for leaves and stem
Yellow or orange crepe paper for the flowers
Scissors
Wire cutter
Ruler
Craft glue or white glue
Brush for applying glue
Floral wire, 28 gauge to wire flower together, 20-gauge for stem
Floral tape (optional)

Cut out pattern pieces or templates

Make the Leaves

1. Cut 6 or more leaves for each marigold, paying attention to grain lines.
2. Cut a 6" piece of 28-gauge wire for each leaf.
3. Use your fingers to make a tiny loop at the end of each wire so you don't stick your fingers, and then straighten the wire to remove any "bumps."
4. Apply a bead of glue down the center of a leaf.
5. Lay a piece of wire on the glue and use the brush to smooth it down.
6. Let the leaf dry before you use it.
7. Repeat steps 4 through 7 for each leaf.

> **Note: More experienced flower makers may want to use the leaf "sandwich" technique as described in the instructions for Tulip.**

Make the Center of the Flower

1. From yellow or orange crepe paper, cut a strip 2" wide (measure with the grain) and 5' long (against the grain). If you use a streamer, just measure off 5' and cut.
2. Cut a 6" length of 28-gauge wire to hold the center together, and an 8" length of 20-gauge wire for the stem. Use your fingers to make tiny loops at each end for safety. Straighten the wires.
3. Hold one short end of the strip at the top in your left hand between thumb and forefinger. Hold the top of the strip about and inch to the right with your right hand.
4. Pull gently to stretch the top of the crepe paper strip.
5. Move your fingers so your left hand is where the right hand was and your right hand is another inch to the right.
6. Repeat steps 4 and 5 all along the top of the 5' strip to the end.
7. Glue the top inch of the 20-gauge wire and lay the glued end of the wire on one end of the fluted 5' strip, so it parallels the grain of the paper.
8. Bit by bit, gather the strip around the wire, keeping the wire in the center. Use glue as needed.
9. Wrap the base of the center with the 28-gauge wire to secure and wind any excess wire around the stem.

Assemble the Flower

1. Cut a 1" wide strip of green crepe paper, about 3' long (or use floral tape).
2. Dab a little glue on the base of the flower, where it is wrapped with wire.
3. Using the 1" strip of green crepe paper, wrap it around the 20-gauge wire to form the stem as described in Chapter 1. Begin by wrapping the glued base of the flower.
4. Add leaves by wrapping the wire around the stem. Add leaves in pairs on opposite sides of the stem, beginning about 2" below the base of the flower, and then leave about 1" between each pair of leaves.

POINSETTIA

Attach a number of these poinsettias to a real or imitation evergreen garland, using the flower stems to attach them to the garland. Use garlands over windows and doors for a beautiful, yet inexpensive, winter decoration. Poinsettias can also be used flat, to decorate a mirror or picture frame, for instance. The flowers can be waxed or hair-sprayed. If your poinsettia flowers will be seen "up close and personal," we recommend using the artificial stamens you can find at any crafts store.

You will need:

Green crepe paper for leaves and stem
Yellow crepe paper for center and stamens
Red crepe paper for the poinsettias
Scissors
Wire cutter
Ruler
Craft glue or white glue
Brush for applying glue
Floral wire, 20 gauge for stems, 28 gauge to wire flower together
Floral tape (optional)
Artificial stamens (optional)
Cut out pattern pieces or templates

Make the Petals

1. From the red paper, cut 3 small (pattern No. 1), 4 medium (pattern No.2) and 6 large (Pattern No. 3) petals for each poinsettia, paying attention to the grain marks. Cut each petal separately; the flower will look more natural if the petals are not exactly alike.
2. For each petal:
   - Cut a piece of 28-gauge wire long enough to fit down the center of the petal from the pointed tip to the base of the petal.
   - Make a thin bead of glue down the center of each petal.
   - Lay the wire on the glue and gently smooth it down with your finger.
3. Set the petals aside, glued side up, until the glue is clear and dry. You need not weight them down.

Make the Leaves:

1. Cut 4 10" pieces of 28-gauge wire, straighten it to remove the "bumps," and use your fingers to make a tiny loop at each end to prevent poking yourself.
2. From the green crepe paper, cut a strip 1/2" wide (with the grain) and at least 2' long to wrap the leaf stems.

3. From the green crepe paper, cut 8 leaf shapes to make 4 finished leaves, paying attention to the grain marks. Cut each leaf shape separately.
4. Make a leaf by sandwiching wire between 2 leaf shapes. Repeat these steps for each leaf:
    - Make a thin line of glue down the middle of one leaf shape from the top of the shape to the bottom.
    - Lay the wire on the glue, with the extra wire sticking out of the flat bottom of the leaf shape.
    - Lay the second leaf shape top of the first one, carefully matching the sides.
    - Weight the leaf-wire-leaf "sandwich" with a heavy book and let the glue dry for a few minutes.
    - Little by little, lift the sides of the top leaf shape and apply a line of glue to the outer edge of the bottom leaf shape.
    - Carefully press the top leaf shape to the bottom one, making sure the edges match. If the edges do not match, trim with your scissors.
    - Weight the leaf-wire-leaf "sandwich" again and let it dry.
    - Wrap the stem with green floral tape or with a 1" wide strip of green crepe paper as described in Chapter 1.

Make the Center of the Flower

1. From red crepe paper, cut three narrow triangles 2" high (measure with the grain) and 1/4" wide at the base (measure against the grain). Twist the pointed end about 3/4" from the point, making an upside down "U."
2. Cut a 6" length of 28-gauge wire to hold the center together, and a 14" length of 20-gauge wire for the stem. Use your fingers to make tiny loops at each end for safety. Straighten the wires.

> *Note: If you are using artificial stamens, skip the next 3 steps.*

3. Cut one piece of green and one piece of yellow crepe paper, each measuring 2" high (with the grain) and 4" wide (against the grain).
4. Gently stretch the green and yellow paper, holding one 2" end in each hand, until it looses all its "give."
5. Put the green piece on top of the yellow one. Cut straight lines 1/8" apart and 1" deep along the 4" side to make the fringe.
6. Apply glue to the top 1" of the 14" length of 20-gauge wire.

7. If you made your own stamens, lay the glued end of the wire on one end of the strip of green fringe. Gather the uncut edge of the fringe into a bunch, inserting the three twisted pieces of red paper so the twists are on top of the fringed side. If you use artificial stamens, gather them around the glued end of the wire.
8. Add the 3 red triangles, evenly spaced, around the bunch of stamens, with the bent tip on the top.
9. Wrap the base of the center with the 28-gauge wire to secure and trim any excess.

Assemble the Flower

1. Cut a 1" strip of green crepe paper, using the whole package as described in Chapter 1.
2. Cut a 10" length of 28-gauge (fine) wire. Make a tiny loop at each end of the wire for safety.
3. Glue the 3 small petals to the flower center, spacing them evenly. The wired side should face the outside of the flower.
4. Glue the 4 medium petals to the flower center, spacing them evenly.
5. Do the same thing to 6 remaining petals, so they are evenly spaced around the center.
6. Using the 10" length of 28-gauge (fine) wire, tightly wrap the bottom inch or so of the flower and continue wrapping down the 20-gauge wire stem.
7. Using the 1" strip of green crepe paper, wrap it around the 20-gauge wire at the stem until it is about 1/4" thick. Continue wrapping down the wire to form the stem as described in Chapter 1.
8. Wrap again, using floral tape if you have it, or more 1" wide green crepe paper, adding the first leaves about 2" from the bottom of the flower on opposite sides of the stem and the next pair 2" below that.
9. Shape the flower:
    - Holding the stem at the base of the flower, bend each petal, working from the outside to the inside to form a flattened flower.
    - Still holding the stem, run your finger along the underside of each petal from the center to the tip, to give the petals dimension. If necessary, bend the tips of the red triangles in the center of the flower down again.
    - Bend the leaves out from the stem.

> **Note: If you will use the flower flat, cut the stem to about four inches and coil it around the base of the flower as a support or use it to attach the flower to a wreath.**

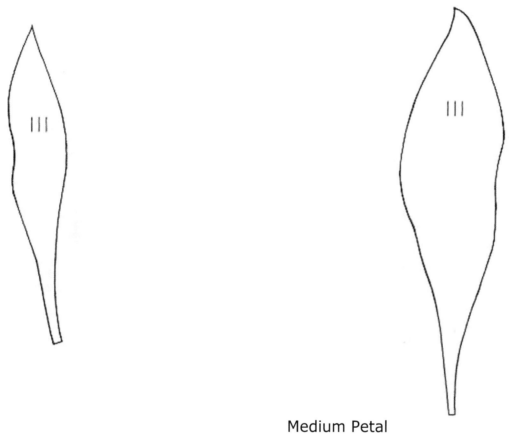

Small Petal

Medium Petal

The Art of Making Paper Flowers

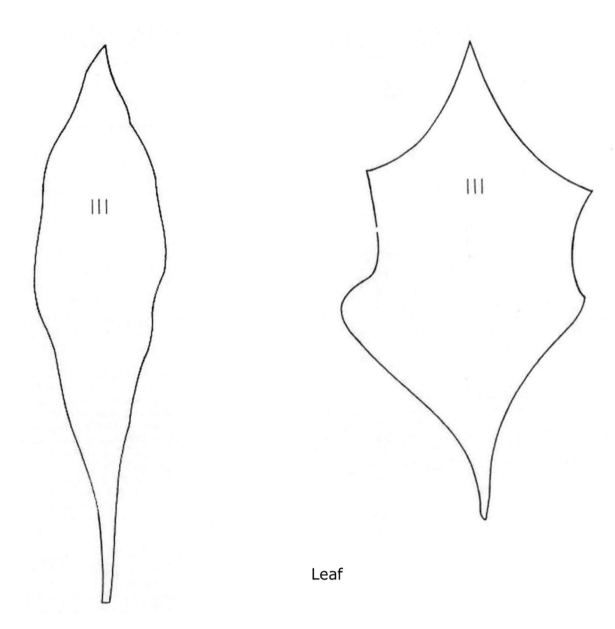

Leaf

Large Petal

MEMORIAL DAY POPPY

The Memorial Day poppy is meant to adorn a buttonhole or lapel. It is also known as the Flanders poppy. It has no leaves. For a patriotic touch, use blue crepe paper rather than black and use a strip of white crepe paper to replace the green in the center fringe. If you decide to use these poppies in a bouquet, you can use the leaf pattern and related instructions from the Oriental Poppy.

You will need:

Green crepe paper for center and stem
Black crepe paper for center and stamens
Red crepe paper for the poppies
Scissors
Cutter for wire
Ruler
Craft glue or white glue
Brush for applying glue
Floral wire, 28 gauge to wire flower together

The Art of Making Paper Flowers 48

Stem wire 20 gauge
Floral tape (optional)
Cut out pattern pieces or templates

Make the Center of the Flower

1. Cut small strips of black crepe paper to make 1/4" ball (or use scraps of crepe paper).
2. Cut a piece of black crepe paper about 1-1/2" square.
3. Cut a 6" length of 28-gauge wire to hold the center together, and an 8" length of 20-gauge wire for the stem. Use your fingers to make tiny loops at each end for safety. Straighten the wires.
4. Make a ball of the crepe paper about 1/4" in diameter:

   - Roll and squeeze the small strips or scraps into a ball. Roll between the palms of your hands, as you would cookie dough.
   - Glue the loop on the heavy (20-gauge) wire.
   - Gently open the ball slightly and insert the glued loop.
   - Hold the ball with the wire tightly for a few seconds to allow the glue to set.
   - Glue any outer edges of the ball that do not lay flat.
   - Flatten the top of the ball by pushing it down on your work surface. It should be about 1/4" thick.

5. Stretch the 1-1/2" black square over the top of the ball, bring it down around the sides of the ball, and fasten with glue at the bottom. The top should be smooth, but the sides will be covered so they can look "rough."
6. Make a fringe to serve as stamens:

   - From black crepe paper, cut a strip 1-1/2" wide (measure with the grain) and 1" long (against the grain).
   - From green crepe paper, cut a strip 1-1/2" wide (measure with the grain) and 1" long.
   - Put the piece of green crepe paper on top of the piece of black crepe paper and gently stretch them against the grain, holding one 1-1/2" side in each hand.
   - Keeping the two colors of paper together, fold them in half to 3/4" wide (with the grain).
   - Cut straight lines 1/2" deep with the grain and as close together as you can to make the fringe.

7. Wrap the fringe around the bottom of the ball, with the green side next to the ball, so about 3/8" of fringe sticks up above the ball.
8. Wrap the base of the center with the 28-gauge wire to secure and wind any excess wire around the stem.

Make the Petals

1. From the red paper, cut 2 petals for each poppy.
2. Ruffle the outside edge of each petal:

   - With the grain of the paper vertical, hold the outside edge of the top of one petal in both hands with your thumbs and forefingers. Your left hand should be at 10 o'clock; your right hand at 12 o'clock. You should be able to see about 1" of crepe paper between your thumbs.
   - Gently pull the paper. You have a stretched part, and an unstretched part (the part where you were holding the crepe paper).
   - Move your hands so your left thumb and forefinger are at 12 o'clock (where your right hand was) and your right hand is at 2 o'clock.
   - Gently pull the paper.
   - Repeat on the opposite side of the flower.
   - Ruffle the other petal in the same way.

3. Cut a tiny hole at the center of the circular petal.

Assemble the Flower

1. Cut a 1/2" wide strip of green crepe paper, about a foot long.
2. Cut a 6" length of 28-gauge (fine) wire. Make a tiny loop at each end of the wire for safety.
3. Put one petal on top of the other, so the ruffled sides do not overlap.
4. Dab a little glue near the hole in the top flower.
5. Slide the petals up the stem and push them against the stamens.
6. Using the 6" length of 28-gauge (fine) wire, tightly wrap the bottom inch or so of the flower.
7. Wrap the ends of the 28-gauge wire around the 20-gauge wire.

8. Using the 1/2" strip of green crepe paper, wrap it around the 20-gauge wire to form the stem as described in Chapter 1.

Petal

ORIENTAL POPPY

When I was a child, we enlarged this pattern until we had flowers about 8" across and sprayed them with hairspray for a porcelain-like finish. Mom put them in a tall cylinder vase. They brightened a corner of our living room for a long time.

You will need:

Green crepe paper for center and stem
Black crepe paper for center and stamens
Orange or red crepe paper for the poppies
Scissors
Wire cutter
Ruler
Craft glue or white glue
Brush for applying glue
Floral wire, 28gauge to wire flower together, 20 gauge for stem
Floral tape (optional)
Cotton ball about 1/2" across (optional)

Cut out pattern pieces or templates

Make the Center of the Flower

1. Cut a 3-1/2" square from one end of the strip.
2. From green crepe paper, cut a strip 1-1/2" wide (measure with the grain) and 1" long.
3. Cut pieces from the black crepe strip to make a 1/2" ball (or use scraps of crepe paper or a cotton ball).
4. Cut a 6" length of 28-gauge wire to hold the center together, and an 8" length of 20-gauge wire for the stem. Use your fingers to make tiny loops at each end for safety. Straighten the wires.
5. Make a ball of black crepe paper about 1/2" in diameter (you need only glue and insert the wire if you use a cotton ball):

- Roll and squeeze the small strips or scraps into a ball. Roll between the palms of your hands, as you would cookie dough.
- Glue the loop on the heavy (20-gauge) wire.
- Gently open the ball slightly and insert the glued loop.
- Hold the ball with the wire tightly for a few seconds to allow the glue to set.
- Glue any outer edges of the ball that do not lay flat.

6. Cover the ball:

   - Lay the 3-1/2" black square on your work surface.
   - Dab glue on each corner of the square.
   - Put the ball in the center of the square and hold the wire vertical.
   - Pull one glued corner across the ball; twist it around the wire; and add a dab of glue to secure it.
   - Pull the diagonally opposite corner across the ball; twist it around the wire and secure it with glue.
   - Pull each remaining corner a across and secure.
   - Working from the top to the bottom of the ball, gently twist all the corners around the wire.
   - Smooth and flatten the top of the ball by rubbing it on your work surface. The sides will be hidden so they can look "rough."

Note: If you are using artificial stamens, skip steps 7 and 8. Cut each double stamen in half, glue at the bottom (the cut end) and attach around the black ball.

7. Make a fringe to serve as stamens:

   - From black crepe paper, cut a strip 1-1/4" wide (measure with the grain) and 15" long (against the grain).
   - Fold the strip to a manageable length and stretch gently against the grain, holding one 1-1/4" side in each hand.
   - You will make a fringe from the stretched paper. Cut straight lines 3/4" deep (parallel to the grain) and 1/8" apart.
   - Moisten your fingers, then roll the cut pieces of fringe between your fingers so they look like tiny spikes. These will be the stamens.

The Art of Making Paper Flowers

8. Holding the center by the wire, with the ball hanging down, wrap the fringe of stamens around it, gluing as needed. The stamens should be about 3/4" above the top of the ball.
9. Wrap the base of the flower center with 28-gauge wire to secure; continue wrapping the wire down the stem.

Make the Leaves

1. From green crepe paper, cut a strip 1" wide (with the grain) and at least 3' long (against the grain).
2. From the green paper, cut 4 leaf shapes for each poppy, paying attention to the grain lines.
3. Cut 2 - 10" pieces of 28-gauge wire. Straighten each piece and make a tiny loop at each end to avoid poking yourself.
4. Make a leaf by sandwiching wire between 2 leaf shapes. Repeat these steps for each leaf:

   - Make a thin line of glue down the middle of one leaf shape from the top of the shape to the bottom.
   - Lay the wire on the glue, with the extra wire sticking out of the flat bottom of the leaf shape.
   - Lay the second leaf shape top of the first one, carefully matching the sides.
   - Weight the leaf-wire-leaf "sandwich" with a heavy book and let the glue dry for a few minutes.
   - Little by little, lift the sides of the top leaf shape and apply a line of glue to the outer edge of the bottom leaf shape.
   - Carefully press the top leaf shape to the bottom one, making sure the edges match. If the edges do not match, trim with your scissors.
   - Weight the leaf-wire-leaf "sandwich" again and let it dry.
   - Wrap the stem with green floral tape or with a 1" wide strip of green crepe paper as described in Chapter 1.

Make the Petals

1. From the orange or red paper, cut 4 petals for each poppy, paying attention to the grain marks.
2. Ruffle the outside edge of each petal:

   - With the grain of the paper vertical, hold the outside edge of the top of one petal in both hands with your thumbs and forefingers. Your left hand should be at 10 o'clock; your right hand at 12 o'clock. You should be able to see about 1" of crepe paper between your thumbs.
   - Gently pull the paper. You have a stretched part, and an unstretched part (the part where you were holding the crepe paper).
   - Move your hands so your right thumb and forefinger are at 10 o'clock (where your right hand was) and your right hand is at 8 o'clock.
   - Gently pull the paper.
   - Now ruffle the other half of the flower, with your left hand at 12 o'clock and your right hand at 2 o'clock, and then with your left hand at 2 o'clock and right hand at 4 o'clock.
   - Ruffle the other petals in the same way.

Assemble the Flower

1. Cut a 1" wide strip of green crepe paper, using the whole packet as described in Chapter 1.
2. Cut a 10" length of 28-gauge (fine) wire. Make a tiny loop at each end of the wire for safety and straighten the wire.
3. Holding the flower center upside down by the wire, glue one petal to the flower center so the top of the flower is 1-1/2" above the center. The petal should "cup" around the center. Hold the petal until the glue sets.
4. Glue another petal opposite the first.
5. Glue the other petals so they overlap the first two.
6. Using the 10" length of 28-gauge (fine) wire, tightly wrap the bottom inch or so of the flower and continue to wrap down the 20-gauge wire.
7. Using the 1" strip of green crepe paper, wrap it around the 20-gauge wire to form the stem as described in Chapter 1.
8. Wrap the stem again, using floral tape if you have it, adding the first leaf 4" from the bottom of the flower, and the second leaf 4" below the first.
9. Shape and stretch the petals to make a natural-looking poppy.

Petal

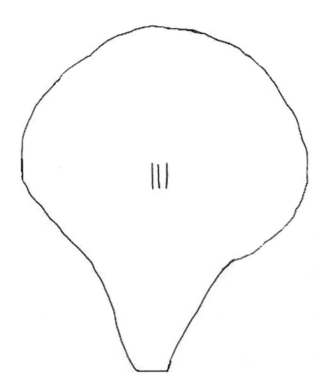

Leaf

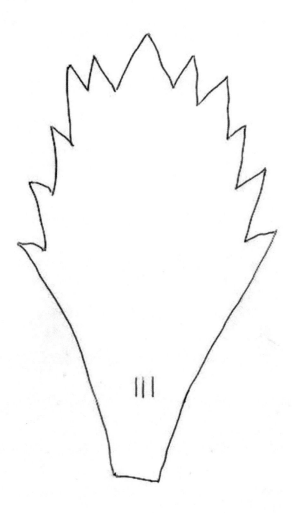

CRUSHED ROSE

These small roses are not terribly realistic, but they are lovely used as corsages or small arrangements. You can glue them to a place card, or use them as decoration for small packages. The instructions will give you several mini-roses. If you make a boutonniere, omit the leaves and make the stem about 3" long.

You will need:

Green crepe paper for leaves and stem
Colored or white crepe paper for the roses
Scissors
Wire cutter
Ruler
Knitting needle, medium sized, not plastic
Craft glue or white glue
Brush for applying glue
Floral wire, 20 gauge for stems, 28 gauge to wire flower together
Floral tape (optional)
Pattern or template to make leaves.

Make the Leaves and Calyx:

1. Cut 1 or 2 leaves for each rose you make, cut 2 leaf pieces at a time.
2. Cut 2 pieces of 28 gauge wire 3" long. Sandwich the wire between 2 of the leaf shapes, glue together.
3. Cut a piece of green crepe paper 1" wide (with the grain) and 3" long (against the grain).
4. Cut to make 3 strips of fringe 1" long, cut each strip 1/2" deep and 1/4" apart. This is your calyx.

Note: If you can, simply cut the strip so each piece of fringe is pointed. Then you will not need to snip the fringe to make points.

The Art of Making Paper Flowers

5. Snip each piece of the fringe so that it is pointed at the top.

Make the Flower

1. Cut a piece of 28-gauge wire about 2" longer than you want the finished stem.
2. Straighten the wire and make a tiny loop at each end for safety.
3. From the flower-colored crepe paper, a strip 5-6" wide (with the grain) and 5" long (against the grain). If you would like the flower to be fuller make it 10"-12" wide (with the grain).
4. If you are not using floral tape, cut a strip of green crepe paper for the stem, about ½" wide (with the grain) and 2' long.
5. Smoothly roll the crepe paper around the knitting needle, so the grain of the paper is along the length of the needle.
6. Push the crepe paper together from both ends.
7. Carefully remove the whole "scrunched tube" of crepe paper from the needle.
8. Cut off pieces of the tube, each 1-1/2" long.
9. Use each piece to make a rose:
    - Carefully unroll the piece, then roll it up again loosely.
    - Pinch the bottom of the roll together to make the base of the flower.
    - Wrap one end of the wire around the base to hold it. The remaining wire will be the stem.
    - Glue the bottom of the calyx fringe and wrap it around the base of the bud.
    - Using floral tape or green crepe paper, wrap the stem, adding leaves where you like them.

LARGE ROSE

Arrange these roses in a vase, or make a shorter stem, add the leaves directly below the rose and use as a corsage. Mix with smaller roses in a bouquet. Add rose buds, perhaps in a lighter shade to the stems of some of the roses.

The Art of Making Paper Flowers

You will need:

Green crepe paper for leaves or artificial rose-leaf sprays (3 or 4 per flower)
You chosen color of crepe paper for the flowers
Scissors
Wire cutter
Ruler
Pencil
White glue or craft glue
Brush for applying glue
Florist's wire, 20 gauge for stems, 28 gauge to wire flower together
Floral tape, green (optional)
Cut out pattern pieces or templates

Make the Leaf Sprays

Skip these steps if you will use artificial rose-leaf sprays. You will need 3 or 4 leaf sprays for each flower.

> ***Note: Because you need so many leaves to make a rose stem, this is a good time to use the technique for cutting out several pieces described in Chapter 1***

1. From the green crepe paper, cut 2 large leaves and 4 small leaves for each spray, paying attention to the grain lines. For 3 sprays, you will need 3 large and 6 small leaves.
2. Cut a strip of green crepe paper 1/2" wide (with the grain) across the whole packet of crepe paper to use for wrapping stems (or use floral tape).
3. Cut one 7" piece and two 5" pieces of fine (28-gauge) wire.
4. Straighten each piece and add a small loop each end for safety.
5. Make the large leaf:
   - Apply a thin bead of glue from top to bottom of one large leaf shape.
   - Lay the 7" wire along the glue so it sticks out from the bottom of the leaf.
   - Apply a thin bead of glue near the outside of the leaf.
   - Gently place the second leaf on top to make a sandwich.

6. Make the small leaves:
   - Apply a thin bead of glue from top to bottom of two of the small leaf shapes.
   - Lay a 5" piece of wire on each.
   - Apply glue near the outside of each leaf.
   - Place a second leaf shape on top of each glued leaf.
7. Beginning at the base of the large leaf, wrap the stem with green crepe paper or floral tape. Add the two small leaves opposite each other about 1" below the base of the large leaf.

Make the Calyx

1. From green crepe paper, cut the calyx, paying attention to the grain lines.
2. Roll the tip of each point between your thumb and forefinger.

Note: You can give the leaves and calyx a more shiny, realistic finish by spraying them with hairspray. Use several light coats, and let the pieces dry between coats.

Make the Petals

If you are making several roses, use a petal or two more or less on some of them. The petals are shaped so that some look more open, some look still unfurled. In a bouquet of natural roses, you would have some with more of the open petals, some with most of the petals still unfurled.

You will need 19 petals for each rose. You will decide how many of each group you want to make. To make flowers that are just beginning to open, use mostly Group 1 and Group 2 petals.

1. From the rose-colored crepe paper, cut 19 petals, paying attention to the grain lines.
2. Shape the petals:

   Group 1 – Unfurled – Make 5

   - Holding each petal between your thumb and forefinger at the widest part, pull gently until the petal has a deep

The Art of Making Paper Flowers

indentation (cup). The indentation will be on the outside of the flower.

- Hold the top of the petal with the thumb and forefinger of your left hand about 1/4" left of the center and the thumb and forefinger of your, right hand, pull gently to make a slight flute in the petal edge.

Group 2 – Beginning to open – Make 5

- Holding each petal between your thumb and forefinger just below the top of the petal, pull gently until the petal has a deep indentation (cup). The indentation will be on the outside of the flower.

- Curl each petal by holding it at the bottom between your thumb and forefinger and pulling it gently across the back of your closed scissors. The curl will face away from the center of the flower.

Group 3 – Open – Make 9

- Curl each petal by wrapping the top around a pencil. The curl will face away from the center of the flower.

- Holding each petal between your thumb and forefinger just below the widest part, pull gently until the petal has a slight indentation (cup) (less indented than for Group 2). The indentation will be on the outside of the flower.

Assemble Each Flower

1. Cut a 1/2" wide (with the grain) strip of green crepe paper across the whole packet of paper as described in Chapter 1 to use to wrap the stem.
2. Cut a 12-15" piece of heavy (20-gauge) wire; cut a 10" piece of fine (28-gauge) wire. Straighten the wires and make a tiny loop at each end for safety.
3. Make the rose:

    - Make the center with a Group 1 petal, by rolling it around on itself into a loose cylinder.

- Glue 1" of one end of the heavy (20-gauge) wire.
- Insert the wire into the center of the cylinder to make the stem. Wrap the bottom of the petal around the wire and twist it to secure.
- Hold the flower by the wire, with the central cylindrical petal facing down when you add the remaining petals and the calyx.
- Add 4 more Group 1 petals around the center, overlapping each one about half way across the previous petal. Fasten each with a dab of glue on the petal. Stagger each row slightly.
- Add the petals in Group 2 in a row around the center, then Group 3 in its own row, not overlapping as much, and with each row slightly higher than the last.
- Secure the petals by wrapping the base of the flower with 28-gauge wire.
- Apply a bead of glue to the solid base of the green calyx.
- Wrap the calyx around the base of the flower.
- Fasten the calyx by wrapping the 28-gauge wire around the base of the flower.

4. Using the green crepe paper or floral tape, wrap the stem as described in Chapter 1.
5. Wrap the stem a second time, adding the leaf sprays on opposite sides of the stem about 2" below the flower for the first stem, and the rest 2-1/2" apart.
6. Bend the points of the calyx down and away from the flower and use a dab of glue to affix 1 or 2 of them to the base of the flower.
7. Bend the flower in the direction you want it to face.
8. Bend the leaves away from the stem.

Large Leaf

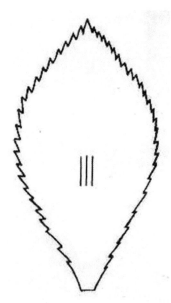

Small Leaf

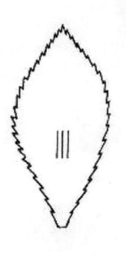

Calyx

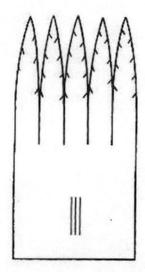

The Art of Making Paper Flowers

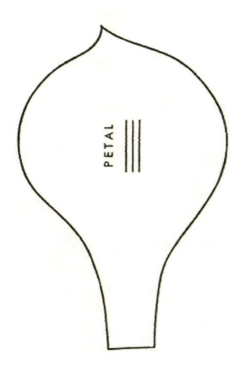

Petal

ROSE

Arrange these roses in a vase, or make a shorter stem, add the leaves directly below the rose and use as a corsage. Go wild with color and make roses you would never see in nature, but that compliment your décor perfectly.

You will need:

Green crepe paper for leaves or artificial rose-leaf sprays (3 or 4 per flower)
You chosen color of crepe paper for the flowers
Scissors
Wire cutter
Ruler
Pencil

The Art of Making Paper Flowers

White glue or craft glue
Brush for applying glue
Florist's wire, 20 gauge for stems, 28 gauge to wire flower together
Floral tape, green (optional)
Cut out pattern pieces or templates

Make the Leaf Sprays

Skip these steps if you will use artificial rose-leaf sprays. You will need 3 or 4 leaf sprays for each flower.

> ***Note: Because you need so many leaves to make a rose stem, this is a good time to use the technique for cutting out several pieces described in Chapter 1.***

1. From the green crepe paper, cut 2 large leaf and 4 small leaves for each spray, paying attention to the grain lines. For 3 sprays, you will need 3 large and 6 small leaves.
2. Cut a strip of green crepe paper 1/2" wide (with the grain) across the whole packet of crepe paper to use for wrapping stems (or use floral tape).
3. Cut one 7" piece and two 5" pieces of fine (28-gauge) wire.
4. Straighten each piece and add a small loop each end for safety.
5. Make the large leaf:
   - Apply a thin bead of glue from top to bottom of one large leaf shape.
   - Lay the 7" wire along the glue so it sticks out from the bottom of the leaf.
   - Apply a thin bead of glue near the outside of the leaf.
   - Gently place the second leaf on top to make a sandwich.
6. Make the small leaves:
   - Apply a thin bead of glue from top to bottom of two of the small leaf shapes.
   - Lay a 5" piece of wire on each.
   - Apply glue near the outside of each leaf.
   - Place a second leaf shape on top of each glued leaf.
7. Beginning at the base of the large leaf, wrap the stem with green crepe paper or floral tape. Add the two small leaves opposite each other about 1" below the base of the large leaf.

Make the Calyx

From green crepe paper, cut the calyx, paying attention to the grain lines.
Roll the tip of each point between your thumb and forefinger.

> **Note: Give the leaves and calyx a more shiny, realistic finish by spraying them with hairspray. Use several light coats, and let the pieces dry between coats.**

Make the Petals

If you are making several roses, use a petal or two more or less on some of them. The petals are shaped so that some look more open, some look still unfurled. In a bouquet of natural roses, you would have some with more of the open petals, some with most of the petals still unfurled.

You will need about 15 petals for each rose. You will decide how many of each group you want to make. To make flowers that are just beginning to open, cut the pattern about 1/8" smaller all around and use mostly Group 1 and Group 2 petals.

1. From the rose-colored crepe paper, cut 15 petals, paying attention to the grain lines.
2. Shape the petals:

   Group 1 – Unfurled – Make 5

   - Holding each petal between your thumb and forefinger near the top, pull gently until the petal has a deep indentation (cup). The indentation, the "bottom of the cup," will be on the outside of the flower.

   Group 2 – Beginning to open – Make 4 or 5

   - Holding each petal between your thumb and forefinger at the widest part, pull gently until the petal has an indentation (cup) (less indented than for Group 1). The indentation will be on the outside of the flower.

- Curl each petal by holding it at the bottom between your thumb and forefinger and pulling it gently across your closed scissors. You may need to repeat the process to create a nice curl. The curl will face away from the center of the flower.

- *Group 3 – Almost open – Make 4 or 5*

- Holding each petal between your thumb and forefinger at the widest part, pull gently until the petal has a slight indentation (cup) (less indented than for Group 2). The indentation will be on the outside of the flower.

- Curl each petal by wrapping it around a pencil. Wrap the top of the petal around the pencil and continue wrapping to the bottom. The curl will face away from the center of the flower.

Group 4 – Open – Make 2 or 3

- Curl each petal by the top wrapping it around a pencil. The curl will face away from the center of the flower.

- Holding each petal between your thumb and forefinger just below the top, pull gently until the petal has a slight indentation (cup) (less indented than for Group 2). This indentation will be on the outside of the flower.

- Turn the petal so the outside is facing you. Holding each petal between your thumb and forefinger at the widest part of the petal, pull gently until the petal has a slight indentation (cup) (less indented than for Group 2). This indentation will be on the inside of the flower.

Assemble Each Flower

1. Cut a 1/2" wide (with the grain) strip of green crepe paper across the whole packet of paper as described in Chapter 1 to use to wrap the stem.
2. Cut a 12-15" piece of heavy (20-gauge) wire; cut a 10" piece of fine (28-gauge) wire. Straighten the wires and make a tiny loop at each end for safety.

3. Make the rose.
    - Make the center with a Group 1 petal, by rolling it around on itself into a loose cylinder.
    - Glue 1" of one end of the heavy (20-gauge) wire.
    - Insert the wire into the center of the cylinder to make the stem. Wrap the bottom of the petal around the wire and twist it to secure.
    - Hold the flower by the wire, with the central cylindrical petal facing down when you add the remaining petals and the calyx.
    - Add 4 more Group 1 petals around the center, overlapping about half way across the previous petal. Fasten each with a dab of glue on the petal. Stagger each row slightly.
    - Add the petals in Group 2 in a row around the center, then Group 3 in its own row, then Group 4, not overlapping as much, and with each row slightly higher than the last.
    - Secure the petals by wrapping the base of the flower with 28-gauge wire.
    - Apply a bead of glue to the solid base of the green calyx.
    - Wrap the calyx around the base of the flower.
    - Fasten the petals and calyx by wrapping the 10" piece of fine wire around the base of the flower.
4. Using the green crepe paper or floral tape, wrap the stem as described in Chapter 1.
5. Wrap the stem a second time, adding the leaf sprays on opposite sides of the stem about 2" below the flower for the first stem, and the rest 2-1/2" apart.
6. Bend the points of the calyx down and away from the flower and use a dab of glue to affix one or two of them to the base of the flower.
7. Bend the flower in the direction you want it to face.
8. Bend the leaves away from the stem.

The Art of Making Paper Flowers 71

Large Leaf

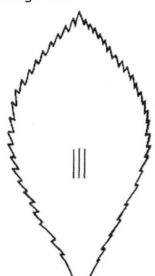

Small Leaf

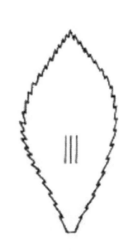

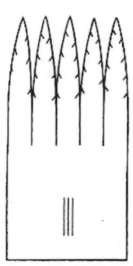

Calyx

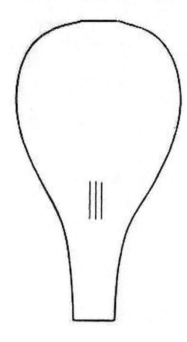

Petal

SHELL FLOWER

Shell flowers are small, and make wonderful additions to corsages or small arrangements. You can glue them to a place card, or use them as decoration for small packages. They are also a good way to use up scraps of crepe paper. The patterns for petals are simply to give you an idea of shape. You can make the petals whatever size you need for the finished flower size you want. You can use the leaf-shape pattern, or make leaves from fringe. Leaves made from the pattern will look nicer on a corsage.

You will need:

Green crepe paper for leaves and stem
Colored or white crepe paper for the shell flowers
Scissors
Wire cutter
Ruler
Craft glue or white glue
Brush for applying glue
Floral wire, 20 gauge for stems, 28 gauge to wire flower together
Floral tape (optional)

Cut out pattern pieces or templates

Make the Leaves:

Note: Either use the pattern given, or use the leaves made from fringe, as you like. You may omit the fringed calyx, but the flower does look better with it.

Either:

    Cut 3 or 4 leaves from the green crepe paper.
    And make 1 fringed strip for the calyx.

Or make 2 strips of fringe as follows, one for the leaves and one for the calyx:

1. Cut a piece of paper 1" wide (with the grain) and 2" long.
2. Cut to make a strip of fringe 2" long with each cut 1/2" deep and 1/4" apart.
3. Snip each piece of the fringe so that it is pointed at the top.

> **Note: If you can cut the strip so each piece of fringe is pointed. Then you will not need to snip the fringe to make points later.**

Make the Flower

1. Cut a piece of 28-gauge wire about 2" longer than you want the finished stem. Straighten the wire and make a tiny loop at each end for safety.
2. If you are not using floral tape, cut a strip of green crepe paper for the stem, about 1/2" wide (with the grain) and 2' long.
3. From the flower-colored crepe paper, cut 1 petal piece for each flower, paying attention to the direction of the grain. Each rounded end of the piece will be the outer edge of a petal.
4. Find the halfway point between the two rounded ends.
5. Gather the crepe paper across the grain at the midpoint. This will be the middle of the flower.
6. Wrap one end of the wire around the gathered center of the flower to hold it. The remaining wire will be the stem.
7. Glue the bottom of the calyx fringe and wrap it around the base of the flower. Wrap with wire to secure and wrap any extra wire around the stem.
8. Using floral tape or green crepe paper, wrap the stem, adding leaves where you like them.
9. Fold the petals up to form the flower, opening the gathered portion at the center, and stretching it slightly.

The Art of Making Paper Flowers

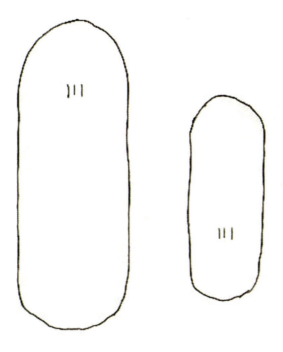

Large Petal   Small Petal

Leaf

TULIPS

Tulips are a springtime flower, brightening our days with their many colors. A bouquet of these tulips will brighten any room, in any season. If you want a tulip that looks like the rare "species" tulips, use the pattern for the inside leaf (the smaller pattern) for all six leaves.

You will need:

Green crepe paper for center, leaves and stem
Black crepe paper for stamens
Any color or colors of crepe paper you choose for the tulips
Scissors
Ruler
White glue or craft glue
Florist's wire, 20 gauge for stems, 28 gauge to wire flower together
Floral tape (optional)
Artificial stamens, preferably black (optional)

Cut out pattern pieces or templates

Make the Leaves:

1. From the green crepe paper, cut 4 leaf shapes for each tulip, paying attention to the grain marks. You will put 2 of them together to make each leaf.
2. Cut 2 10" pieces of 28-gauge wire, straighten each piece to remove the "bumps," and use your fingers to make a tiny loop at each end to prevent poking yourself.
3. Make a leaf by sandwiching wire between 2 leaf shapes. Repeat these steps for each leaf:
    - Make a thin line of glue down the middle of one leaf shape from the top of the shape to the bottom.
    - Lay the wire on the glue, with the extra wire sticking out of the flat bottom of the leaf shape.

- Lay the second leaf shape top of the first one, carefully matching the sides.
- Weight the leaf-wire-leaf "sandwich" with a heavy book and let the glue dry for a few minutes.
- Little by little, lift the sides of the top leaf shape and apply a line of glue to the outer edge of the bottom leaf shape.
- Carefully press the top leaf shape to the bottom one, making sure the edges match. If the edges do not match, trim with your scissors.
- Weight the leaf-wire-leaf "sandwich" again and let it dry.
- Wrap the stem with green floral tape or with a 1" wide strip of green crepe paper as described in Chapter 1.

Make the Center of the Flower

1. Cut an 11" length of 20-gauge (heavy) wire and straighten it. Make a tiny loop at each end of the wire for safety.
2. From green crepe paper, cut a strip 3-1/2" long (against the grain) by 2-1/2" wide (with the grain).
3. Fold the paper so it is 3-1/2" long by 1-1/4" wide.
4. With the folded side up, glue one of the 1-1/4" ends.
5. Lay one end of the wire on the glue so the loop is about 1/2" from the top.
6. Tightly roll the paper around the glued wires to form a cylinder. Now you should have a tight "log" of green crepe paper with wire sticking out of the bottom. The wire will be the stem of the flower.
7. Use glue to hold the log together.

> ***Note: If you are using artificial stamens, cut them in half, glue them to the green "log" and skip the next steps. Cover the outside of the cylinder by gluing on another layer of green crepe paper.***

8. Make the stamens:

    - Cut a strip of black crepe paper 1-1/4" long (against the grain) by 2" wide (with the grain).
    - Beginning your cut at the top of the 2" side of the piece of black crepe paper, cut straight lines with the grain 3/16" apart and 1-1/2" deep along the strip to make 6 sections.

- Use your scissors to round off the top of each section so your strip looks like a picket fence with rounded pickets.
- Starting at the bottom of each cut section, and ending 1/4" from the top, twist each section so your black strip looks like a row of skinny matches with fat heads. Twisting is easier if you moisten your fingertips first.

9. Glue one end of the black strip, then wrap the black strip around the green cylinder. Trim any excess and fasten with glue.

> **Note: The crepe paper stamens do not look very impressive at this point. But they will look just fine when your flower is complete.**

Make the Petals

1. Cut 3 inner petals and 3 outer petals, paying attention to the grain marks.
2. If you want to color the petals, do it now.
3. Hold one petal in both hands with your thumb and forefinger about 1-1/2" from the base of the petal.
4. Gently pull the paper, making it wider to form the "cup-shape" as at the base of real tulip petals.
5. Repeat steps 2 and 3 for the 5 remaining petals.

> **Note: You may find that the petals hold their shape better if you glue a length of the 28-gauge wire to the inside of the petal. If you enlarge the pattern, you will need to make the petals double thickness. Make the same type of "sandwich" petal-wire-petal as you did for the leaves.**

Assemble the Flower

1. Cut a 1" strip of green crepe paper, using the whole package as described in Chapter 1.
2. Cut a 10" length of 28-gauge (fine) wire and straighten it. Make a tiny loop at the ends of the wire for safety.
3. Make a line of glue from the top to the bottom of the green cylinder (the inside of the flower).

4. Using one of the inner petals, hold it with the bowed side facing away from the cylinder and glue the petal to the center cylinder. Be sure the bottom of the petal is at the bottom of the cylinder and attach the petal just up to the bottom of the bowed out portion of the petal.
5. Do the same thing to a second and third inner petal, so they are evenly spaced around the cylinder.
6. Repeat the process with the 3 outer petals, attaching them so they overlap the first round of petals.
7. Using a 10" length of 28-gauge (fine) wire, tightly wrap the bottom inch or so of the flower and continue wrapping down the 20-gauge wire stem.
8. Using the 1" strip of green crepe paper, wrap it around the 20-gauge wire to form the stem as described in Chapter 1.
9. Wrap again, using floral tape if you have it, or more 1" wide green crepe paper, adding the leaves near the bottom of the stem so the top of the leaf is near or below the top of the flower.

Note: You may need to gently stretch the center of each petal so they "cup" nicely around the center.

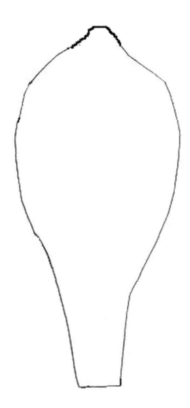

Petal

Leaf

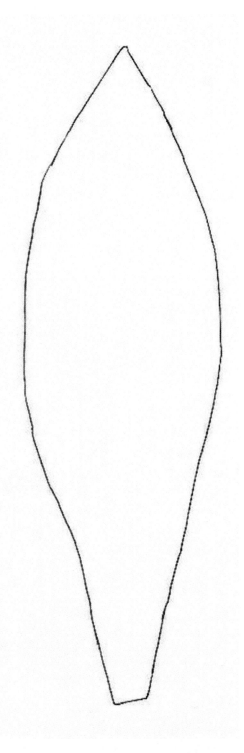

VIOLETS IN A BUNCH

The bunch of violets is quick and easy to make. It makes a simple, but lovely, corsage. This is a good project for children – perhaps at Mother's Day. To make a larger bunch of violets, just use a longer strip of crepe paper. The violets look especially nice if you add some artificial stamens to the bunch. You don't need a stamen for every flower, just a few for effect.

You will need:

Green crepe paper for leaves and stem
Blue, purple or lilac crepe paper for the flowers
Scissors
Wire cutter
Ruler
Craft glue or white glue
Brush for applying glue
Floral wire, 28 gauge to wire flower together, 20-gauge for stem
Floral tape (optional)
Artificial stamens (optional)
Cut out pattern pieces or templates

Note: Use the readily available crepe paper streamers for the flowers. The streamers are already 2" wide.

Make the Leaves:

1. From the green crepe paper, cut 12 leaf shapes to make 6 finished leaves, paying attention to the grain marks. Cut each leaf shape separately.
2. Cut 6 4" pieces of 28-gauge wire, straighten each to remove the "bumps," and use your fingers to make a tiny loop at each end to prevent poking yourself.

3. Make a leaf by sandwiching wire between 2 leaf shapes. Repeat these steps for each leaf:
   - Make a thin line of glue down the middle of one leaf shape from the top of the shape to the bottom.
   - Lay the wire on the glue, with the extra wire sticking out of the flat bottom of the leaf shape.
   - Lay the second leaf shape top of the first one, carefully matching the sides.
   - Weight the leaf-wire-leaf "sandwich" with a heavy book and let the glue dry for a few minutes.
   - Little by little, lift the sides of the top leaf shape and apply a line of glue to the outer edge of the bottom leaf shape.
   - Carefully press the top leaf shape to the bottom one, making sure the edges match. If the edges do not match, trim with your scissors.
   - Weight the leaf-wire-leaf "sandwich" again and let it dry.
   - Wrap the stem with green floral tape or with a 1" wide strip of green crepe paper as described in Chapter 1.

Make the Bunch of Violets

1. Cut a 6" length of 28-gauge wire to hold the center together, and an 8" length of 20-gauge wire for the stem. Use your fingers to make tiny loops at each end for safety. Straighten the wires.
2. From blue or violet crepe paper, cut a strip 2 3/4" wide (measure with the grain) and 2 1/2" long (against the grain). You will need 5 of these strips.
3. Use the petal pattern to cut the petals in the strip. Pull gently to stretch the top of the crepe paper strip.
4. Grab the first petal in the strip about 1" down from the rounded top and twist in a complete circular motion.
5. Repeat step 4 with each petal along the top of each strip of petals to the end.
6. Glue the top inch of the 20-gauge wire and lay the glued end of the wire on one end of the petal strip, so it parallels the grain.
7. Bit by bit, gather the strip around the wire, keeping the wire in the center. Use glue as needed. Add an artificial stamen as you gather for the center of each flower.

> **Note: To add stamens, glue the wire part of the stamens and gather them with the crepe paper, so the top of the stamen is just barely above the top of the flowers.**

8. Make the rest of the petals by just gathering each strip and adding a stamen to each and twisting the bottom of the strip of flowers and gluing to hold together.
9. After you have each strip done then take each petal and curl by gently taking the scissors and curling as you would ribbon only make sure you do this gently so you do not pull off the petal.
10. Take the flower that has the wire surround it with the other flowers, then take 28gauge wire and wrap it around the flowers to hold them together in a bunch any excess wire wrap on stem.

Assemble the Flower

1. Cut a 1" wide strip of green crepe paper, about 3' long.
2. Glue the leaves to the bottom of the bunch of violets, so they make an outer edge for the bunch. Wrap the leaf stem wire around the 20-gauge wire.
3. Dab a little glue on the base of the flower, where it is wrapped with wire.
4. Using the 1" strip of green crepe paper, wrap it around the 20-gauge wire to form the stem as described in Chapter 1. Begin by wrapping the glued base of the flower.
5. Leave a 2-3" stem to accommodate a corsage pin, if desired. Trim any excess stem.

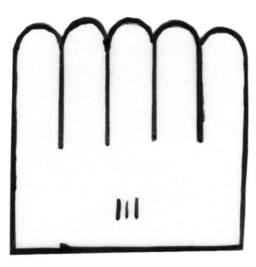

Petals – make a long strip

Leaf

WATER LILY

If you put a water lily on a mirror, it will seem to be floating on a pond. Use either one or three leaves. Add a ceramic frog, and you have a cute centerpiece. Water lilies in nature come in many colors. Try making one in pink, or purple, or even orange. Water lilies are good candidates for the waxing technique.

You will need:

Green crepe paper for leaves and stem
White (or colored) crepe paper for the petals
Amber (or yellow) crepe paper for the flower center
Scissors
Wire cutter
Ruler

Craft glue or white glue
Brush for applying glue
Floral wire, 20 gauge for stems, 28 gauge to wire flower together
Floral tape (optional)
Cotton ball about 1" across (optional)
Cut out pattern pieces or templates

Make the Center of the Flower

1. Cut a 14" length of 20-gauge wire for the stem and a 6" length of 28-gauge wire to hold the center together. Use your fingers to make tiny loops at each end for safety. Straighten the wires.
2. From the amber crepe paper, cut a strip 2-1/2" wide (measure with the grain) across the whole package of crepe paper as described in chapter 1. From the strip, cut a piece 10" long to use for the fringe, and set that piece aside. Cut several smaller pieces from the strip to make a 5/8" ball (or use scraps of crepe paper or a cotton ball).
3. Cut a piece of amber crepe paper 3-1/2" square.
4. Make a ball of amber crepe paper about 5/8" in diameter (you need only glue and insert the wire if you use a cotton ball):

   - Roll and squeeze the small strips or scraps into a ball. Roll between the palms of your hands, as you would cookie dough.
   - Glue the loop on the heavy (20-gauge) wire.
   - Gently open the ball slightly and insert the glued loop.
   - Hold the ball with the wire tightly for a few seconds to allow the glue to set.
   - Glue any outer edges of the ball that do not lay flat.

5. Cover the ball:

   - Lay the 3-1/2" amber square on your work surface.
   - Dab glue on each corner of the square.
   - Put the ball in the center of the square and hold the wire vertical.
   - Pull one glued corner across the ball; twist it around the wire; and add a dab of glue to secure it.
   - Pull the diagonally opposite corner across the ball; twist it around the wire and secure it with glue.
   - Pull each remaining corner a across and secure.

- Working from the top to the bottom of the ball, gently twist all the corners around the wire.
- Smooth and flatten the top of the ball by rubbing it on your work surface. The sides will be hidden so they can look "rough."

6. Make a fringe to serve as stamens:

   - Use the strip you cut in step 2. You should have a strip 2" wide (measure with the grain) and 10" long (against the grain).
   - Fold the strip to a manageable length and stretch gently against the grain, holding one 2" side in each hand until the paper loses its "give."
   - You will make a fringe from the stretched paper. Cut straight lines 1-5/8" deep (parallel to the grain) and 1/8" apart.
   - Gently curl the fringe over your closed scissors, just as you would curl ribbon.

7. Place a bead of glue around the bottom half of the ball.
8. Holding the center by the wire, with the ball hanging down, wrap the fringe of stamens around it, gluing as needed. The stamens should be about 3/4" above the top of the ball.
9. Wrap the base of the flower center with 28-gauge wire to secure; continue wrapping the wire down the stem.

Make the Leaves:

1. From green crepe paper, cut a strip 1" wide (with the grain) and at least 3' long (against the grain).
2. From the green paper, cut 4 leaf shapes for each water lily, paying attention to the grain lines.
3. Cut 4 10" pieces of 28-gauge wire. Straighten each piece and make a tiny loop at each end to avoid poking yourself.
4. Make a leaf by sandwiching wire between 2 leaf shapes. Repeat these steps for each leaf:

   - Make a thin line of glue down the middle of one leaf shape from the top of the shape to the bottom.
   - Lay the wire on the glue, with the extra wire sticking out of the flat bottom of the leaf shape.
   - Lay the second leaf shape top of the first one, carefully matching the sides.

- Weight the leaf-wire-leaf "sandwich" with a heavy book and let the glue dry for a few minutes.
- Little by little, lift the sides of the top leaf shape and apply a line of glue to the outer edge of the bottom leaf shape.
- Carefully press the top leaf shape to the bottom one, making sure the edges match. If the edges do not match, trim with your scissors.
- Weight the leaf-wire-leaf "sandwich" again and let it dry.
- Wrap the stem with green floral tape or with a 1" wide strip of green crepe paper as described in Chapter 1.

Make the Calyx

1. For the calyx, use the petal pattern, but cut from green crepe paper, make four calyx pieces.
2. Hold each calyx piece in both hands and stretch against the grain to form a slightly "cupped" shape. Begin at the top, and work your way down the piece.

Make the Petals

7. Cut 30 petals for each lily, paying attention to the grain lines. Try the technique for cutting many pieces at once described in Chapter 1.
8. Stretch the petals to make a "cup" shape just as you stretched the calyx pieces. The first 7 petals should be rather deeply cupped, the next 10 should be less deeply cupped, and the final 13 petals should be just slightly cupped.

Assemble the Flower

1. Cut a 1" strip of green crepe paper, using the whole package as described in Chapter 1.
2. Cut a 10" length of 28-gauge (fine) wire. Make a tiny loop at each end of the wire for safety and straighten the wire.
3. Add the petals and calyx:

    - Hold the flower center by the wire, so the center hangs upside down.

- Use a brush to apply glue around the bottom half of the center.
- Attach the first deeply cupped petal so it nestles the center in its hollow "cup."
- Attach the 6 remaining deeply cupped petals so they are evenly spaced around the center.
- Use a brush to apply another coat of glue to the bottom half of the flower.
- Affix the 10 less-cupped petals, one at a time, as you attached the first row of petals.
- Apply another coat of glue and attach the third row of petals, in the same way.
- Apply another thin coat of glue and attach the calyx pieces in the same way, evenly spaced around the flower.
- Wrap the base of the flower with the 28-gauge wire to secure.

4. Cut the stem to the desired length.
5. Using the 1" strip of green crepe paper, wrap it around the 20-gauge wire to form the stem as described in Chapter 1.
6. Wrap the stem again, using floral tape if you have it, or more 1" wide green crepe paper. Add the leaves at the bottom of the flower.

> **Note: If the petals get wet from too much glue, just let the flower dry for a few minutes, until it is no longer so sticky.**

The Art of Making Paper Flowers

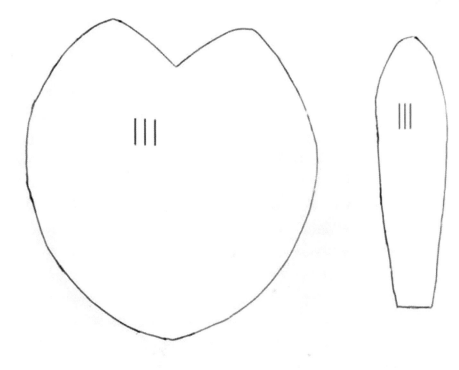

Leaf   Petal

About The Authors

We were both born and raised in a small community along the banks of the Ohio River where there wasn't a lot to do, so you had to find things to keep yourself occupied and stay out of trouble. Thanks to our parents who taught us to use our minds and hands to stay busy, we were able to develop many of the skills and talents that we have today.

We have been in the craft business for over 30 years, in many types of crafts including woodworking, stained glass and a combination of both as in our kitchen cabinets where we put stained glass in our cabinet doors. We also do sewing, Crocheting, mosaics, and flower arrangements both natural and artificial and have also done cake decorating for special occasions.

Over the years there have been many people who have helped us to achieve the talents that we have today. So our goal is to help other people like you to achieve their goals and develop their talents. This is the reason that we have taken on the task of writing the material that we have.

We always want to hear from our customers, so if there is something you would like more information on please contact us at our email address and let us know and we will try to help. robert@ourpaperflowers.com

If you would like to sign up for our Newsletter please go to our website and sign up. Each month we are going to try to keep you updated on the latest news and any new flower designs we have created and other products that we think you might be interested in that will help in your home décor. www.ourpaperflowers.com

We want to thank you for your purchase and we wish you many happy hours of enjoyment with this craft.

Robert and Jane Morris

Made in the USA
Charleston, SC
05 November 2013